FIRST TOUCH SOCCER

NEW YORK
RED BULLS

BY
MARK STEWART

NORWOODHOUSE PRESS

Chicago, Illinois

NorwoodHouse Press

P.O. Box 316598 • Chicago, Illinois 60631
For more information about Norwood House Press please visit our website at
www.norwoodhousepress.com or call 866-565-2900.

Photography and Collectibles:
The trading cards and other memorabilia assembled in the background for this book's cover and interior pages
are all part of the author's collection and are reproduced for educational and artistic purposes.

All photos courtesy of Associated Press except the following individual photos and artifacts (page numbers):
Rob Tringali (4, 8, 15, 18), The Upper Deck Company LLC (6, 11 top), Sports Illustrated for Kids (10 top),
Topps, Inc. (10 bottom, 11 middle & bottom, 16, 22).

Cover image: Rich Graessle/Associated Press

Designer: Ron Jaffe
Series Editor: Mike Kennedy
Content Consultants: Michael Jacobsen and Jonathan Wentworth-Ping
Project Management: Black Book Partners, LLC
Editorial Production: Lisa Walsh

Library of Congress Cataloging-in-Publication Data
Names: Stewart, Mark, 1960 July 7-
Title: New York Red Bulls / By Mark Stewart.
Description: Chicago Illinois : Norwood House Press, 2017. | Series: First
    Touch Soccer | Includes bibliographical references and index. | Audience:
    Age 5-8. | Audience: K to Grade 3.
Identifiers: LCCN 2016058980 (print) | LCCN 2017013337 (ebook) | ISBN
    9781684040841 (eBook) | ISBN 9781599538655 (library edition : alk. paper)
Subjects: LCSH: New York Red Bulls (Soccer team)--Juvenile literature. | New
    York/New Jersey MetroStars (Soccer team)--Juvenile literature.
Classification: LCC GV943.6.N46 (ebook) | LCC GV943.6.N46 S84 2017 (print) |
    DDC 796.334/63097471--dc23
LC record available at https://lccn.loc.gov/2016058980

302N--072017
Manufactured in the United States of America in North Mankato, Minnesota.

CONTENTS

Words in **bold type** are defined on page 24.

The Red Bulls are on the loose after scoring a goal against the Houston Dynamo in 2016.

MEET THE RED BULLS

Soccer has a long history in New York and New Jersey. The two states are neighbors and share many sports teams and fans. This includes the New York Red Bulls. The club has played in New Jersey for more than 20 seasons.

The Red Bulls are known for their world-famous players. They are also known for their goal-scoring. Most of all, they are known for making soccer fun to watch.

TIME MACHINE

In 1996, Major League Soccer (MLS) began its first season. One of the league's first teams was called the New York/New Jersey MetroStars. Later, the club just called itself the MetroStars. In 2006, a company in Austria bought the team and renamed it the New York Red Bulls. The club's great players include Juan Pablo Angel, **Amado Guevara**, ● ⟶ Eddie Pope, and John Wolyniec.

John Wolyniec out-jumps an opponent for a header during a 2008 match.

7

Fans pack the stands for a match against Toronto F.C. in 2016.

BEST SEAT IN THE HOUSE

The Red Bulls moved into a beautiful new soccer stadium in 2010. It is called Red Bull Arena. It is located in Harrison, New Jersey. Red Bull Arena is a short walk from neighborhoods where soccer is the favorite sport. That means the stands are full for almost every match.

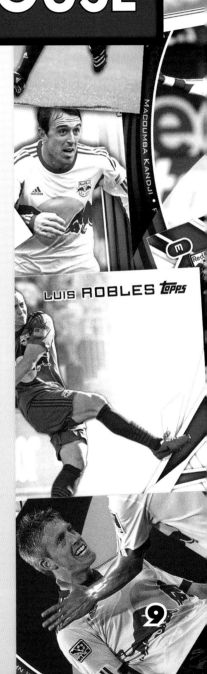

COLLECTOR'S CORNER

These collectibles show some of the best Red Bulls and MetroStars ever.

Clint Mathis
Forward • N.Y./N.J. MetroStars

CLINT MATHIS

Forward/Midfielder
2000–2003 & 2007
Mathis was an exciting scorer. He had seven goals in his first six games with the club.

TIM HOWARD

Goalkeeper
1998–2003
Howard grew up in New Jersey. The fans loved having a hometown star in goal.

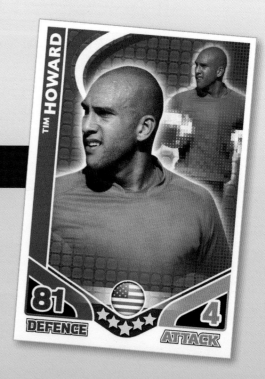

TIM HOWARD
81 DEFENCE
4 ATTACK

JUAN PABLO ANGEL

Forward
2007–2010
Angel was a star in South America and England before joining the Red Bulls. He scored in his first game for New York.

THIERRY HENRY

Forward
2010–2014
Henry made the fans leap out of their seats with his great moves and powerful shot.

BRADLEY WRIGHT-PHILLIPS

Forward
First Year with Club: 2013
Wright-Phillips set a new MLS record with 27 goals in 2014. It was his first full season with the Red Bulls.

WORTHY OPPONENTS

The Red Bulls' main rival is D.C. United. The teams often play three or more times each season. The winner can claim that year's **Atlantic Cup**. In 2015, the Red Bulls began a new rivalry when New York City F.C. joined the league. The teams play less than an hour apart, on either side of the Hudson River.

Mike Grella of the Red Bulls competes for a ball with Patrick Nyarko of D.C. United during a 2016 match.

CLUB WAYS

Fans of the Red Bulls come from all over New York and New Jersey. They drive to Red Bull Arena or take the train. Thousands of fans walk across a bridge from the Ironbound section of Newark. The team sets aside seating sections for different fan clubs. They include the Empire Supporters, Viking Army, and Garden State Ultras. Many fans tailgate before matches.

The fans show their support for the Red Bulls.

ON THE MAP

The Red Bulls bring together players from many countries. These are some of the best:

1 **Clint Mathis** • Conyers, Georgia
2 **Sacha Kljestan** • Huntington Beach, California
3 **Dane Richards** • Montego Bay, Jamaica
4 **Amado Guevara** • Tegucigalpa, Honduras
5 **Juan Pablo Angel** • Medellin, Colombia
6 **Thierry Henry** • Les Ulis, France
7 **Bouna Coundoul** • Dakar, Senegal
8 **Omer Damari** • Rishon LeZion, Israel

SACHA KLJESTAN

MAP OF NORTH AND CENTRAL AMERICA

The Red Bulls' home stadium is in Harrison, New Jersey.

WORLD MAP

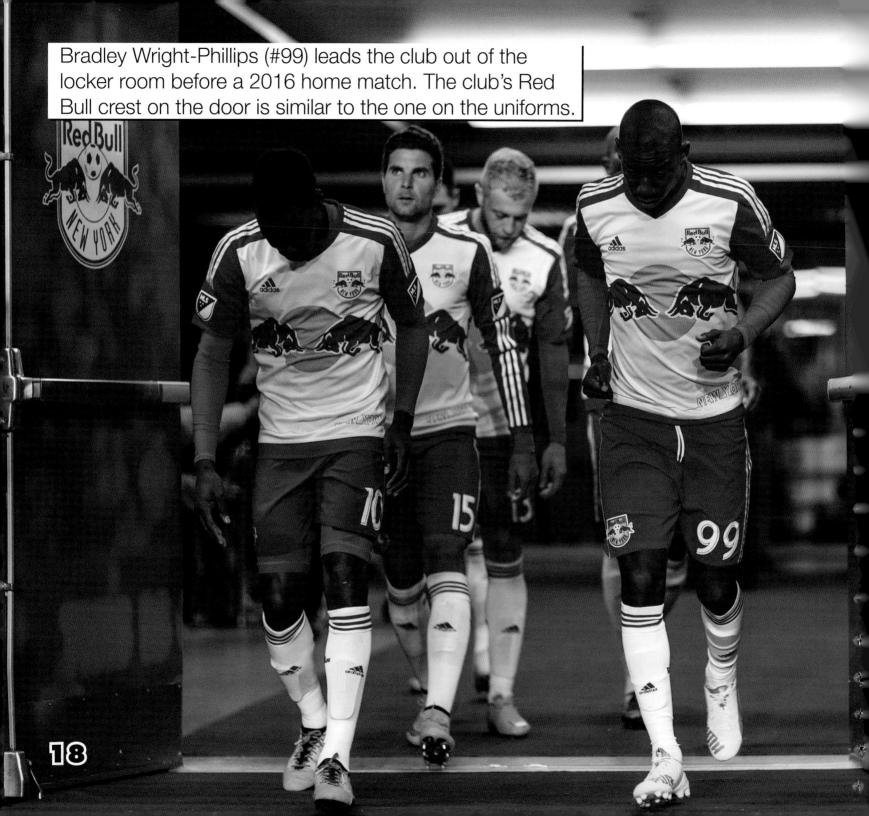

Bradley Wright-Phillips (#99) leads the club out of the locker room before a 2016 home match. The club's Red Bull crest on the door is similar to the one on the uniforms.

KIT AND CREST

Long before the club became the Red Bulls, red was an important team color. Since 2006, its home shirt, shorts, and socks have all been a mix of red and white. The Red Bulls' away **kit** is very different. It usually is blue and yellow. The team's crest shows two red bulls charging each other. It also shows a soccer ball.

We Won!

The Red Bulls' greatest victory came in the 2011 **Emirates Cup**, in England. No one expected the club to do well because three fantastic teams were also in the tournament. New York beat Paris Saint-Germain on the first day, 1–0. The next day, Thierry Henry starred against his old team, Arsenal, in the final. The Red Bulls tied Arsenal 1–1. However, the Red Bulls had more points than the other three teams, which made them Cup champions.

Thierry Henry holds the Emirates Cup after starring against his former team in the 2011 tournament.

FOR THE RECORD

The Red Bulls have won trophies and tournaments in the U.S. and Europe.

Supporters' Shield*

2013

2015

Atlantic Cup**

2003

2010

2011

2013

2015

Emirates Cup

2011

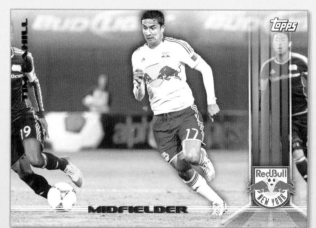

Tim Cahill

* The Supporters' Shield is given to the MLS team with the best record.
** The club was called the MetroStars when it won the Atlantic Cup in 2003.

These stars have won major awards while playing for the Red Bulls:

2001   Tim Howard • MLS Goalkeeper of the Year

2001   Rodrigo Faria • MLS Rookie of the Year

2011   Dwayne DeRosario • MLS Golden Boot*

2013   Thierry Henry • ESPY Best Athlete Award

2014   Tim Cahill • ESPY Best Athlete Award

2014   Bradley Wright-Phillips • MLS Golden Boot

2016   Bradley Wright-Phillips • MLS Golden Boot

DeRosario played for two other teams in 2011.

Soccer Words

Index

Atlantic Cup
A trophy awarded each season to the winner of the series between the Red Bulls and D.C. United. The trophy was created in 2002.

Emirates Cup
A two-day tournament hosted each year by Arsenal F.C. in England. Emirates is the name of the travel company that sponsors the competition.

Kit
The official league equipment of soccer players, including a club's uniform.

Photos are on **BOLD** numbered pages.

About the Author

Mark Stewart has been writing about world soccer since the 1990s, including *Soccer: A History of the World's Most Popular Game*. In 2005, he co-authored Major League Soccer's 10-year anniversary book.

About the New York Red Bulls

Learn more at these websites:
www.newyorkredbulls.com
www.MLSsoccer.com
www.teamspiritextras.com